LAKE GARDA
Travel Guide 2025

A Complete Pocket Guide to Must-See Attractions, Romantic Getaways and Outdoor Adventures for an Unforgettable Italian Escape

Wendy T. Sierra

Copyright

All rights reserved. No part of this book may be reproduced, distributed, or transmitted in any form or by any means, including photocopying, recording, or other electronic or mechanical methods, without the prior written permission of the publisher, except in the case of brief quotations used in reviews or articles.

This book is a work of nonfiction. While every effort has been made to ensure accuracy, the author and publisher assume no responsibility for errors, omissions, or changes in details. Readers are encouraged to verify information independently.

©[2024][Wendy T. Sierra]

Table of Contents

Copyright.. 1
Table of Contents... 2
Forward... 4
Introduction... 6
   Overview of Lake Garda Region........................ 6
   Why Visit Lake Garda in 2025?........................ 8
   Best Time to Visit.. 9
   Local Etiquette and Cultural Tips.................. 10
Getting To Lake Garda............................... 13
Where to Stay in Lake Garda..................... 20
Must-See Attractions................................. 27
   Scaliger Castle in Sirmione............................ 27
   Vittoriale degli Italiani in Gardone Riviera...... 28
   Monte Baldo's Panoramic Views.................... 30
   The Charming Streets of Malcesine................ 31
   Limone sul Garda's Lemon Groves................. 32
Hidden Gems of Lake Garda..................... 35
Fun Things to Do Around Lake Garda........ 41
Dining & Local Cuisine in Lake Garda....... 47
Shopping in Lake Garda............................ 53
Family-Friendly Fun at Lake Garda........... 58
Romantic Experiences at Lake Garda........ 64
Outdoor Adventures on Lake Garda.......... 70
Day Trips From Lake Garda...................... 76

Seasonal Events & Festivals...................... 82
Sustainable Travel Tips for Lake Garda.... 89
Practical Tips for a Smooth Vacation........ 95
Sample Itineraries................................... 101
Conclusion.. 108

Forward

Imagine the sun dipping behind distant hills, casting a golden glow over serene waters as the gentle sound of waves lulls your senses. This was my first memory of Lake Garda, and it has stayed with me ever since. It wasn't just the sheer beauty of the lake that captivated me—it was the feeling of stepping into a world where time seemed to pause, where every corner whispered stories of history, culture, and nature intertwined.

This guide is a labor of love, inspired by my countless visits to this Italian gem. I've explored its bustling towns and hidden hamlets, marveled at its ancient castles, and indulged in its vibrant cuisine. Each trip uncovered a new layer of Lake Garda's charm, and now I'm thrilled to share it all with you.

I'll never forget one particular evening in Sirmione. Wandering through its cobblestone streets, I stumbled upon a small trattoria overlooking the lake. The owner, an elderly gentleman with a kind smile, insisted I try the house specialty—freshly made tortellini drizzled with locally pressed olive oil. As I savored the dish, I listened to his stories about growing up by the lake, his voice brimming with pride and nostalgia. It was a moment of connection, a reminder of how travel isn't just about seeing places but also about meeting people and embracing their way of life.

Lake Garda is a destination that caters to every kind of traveler. Families will find joy in its theme parks and beaches; couples will revel in its romantic vistas; and adventurers will be thrilled by its hiking trails and water sports. Yet, beyond these experiences lies something more profound—a sense of belonging, of being part of something timeless and extraordinary.

This guide is your companion to discovering the magic of Lake Garda. It's filled with practical advice, hidden gems, and personal insights to help you make the most of your journey. But more than that, it's an invitation—to slow down, to immerse yourself in the lake's beauty, and to create your own cherished memories.

So, as you turn the pages, let this be the beginning of your adventure. Lake Garda awaits, ready to welcome you with open arms and endless stories. I promise, it's a place you'll never want to leave—and one you'll always carry in your heart.

Introduction

Lake Garda, a glittering jewel nestled between the breathtaking Dolomite Mountains and northern Italy's undulating plains, has won the hearts of travellers for ages. This beautiful lake, Italy's biggest, features a setting straight out of a storybook: turquoise waters, sun-drenched olive fields, lovely mediaeval villages, and a backdrop of craggy hills. Whether you're looking for a romantic getaway, a family adventure, or a relaxing retreat, Lake Garda has it all: natural beauty, rich culture, and limitless activities.

Allow this guide to accompany you on your journey through this lovely destination. Lake Garda in 2025 promises experiences that will last a lifetime, from discovering hidden jewels to immersing yourself in its ancient customs. Let's look at what makes this place so wonderful!

Overview of Lake Garda Region

Lake Garda is located in three Italian regions: Veneto, Lombardy, and Trentino-Alto Adige, each of which adds its own flavour to the area. Its vastness and various surroundings ensure that there is something for everyone, from lively towns to peaceful getaways.

Northern Lake Garda (Trentino-Alto Adige): The lake's northernmost portion is surrounded by rugged mountains, making it an ideal destination for outdoor lovers. Towns like Riva del Garda have a laid-back attitude and are great for windsurfing, hiking, and cycling.

Eastern Lake Garda (Veneto): Known for its attractive villages such as Bardolino and Lazise, this region is ideal for wine lovers and those looking for romantic seaside promenades.

Southern Lake Garda (Veneto/Lombardy) has undulating hills and historic villages like Sirmione, which is known for its hot springs and old Roman ruins.

Western Lake Garda (Lombardy): You'll discover tranquil beaches, lemon orchards, and artistic communities like Gardone Riviera, which is home to the remarkable Vittoriale degli Italiani estate.

Regardless of where you choose to visit, the region's natural beauty, gastronomic delights, and cultural treasures will enchant you.

Why Visit Lake Garda in 2025?

2025 is shaping up to be an excellent year to visit Lake Garda. Whether you're a first-timer or a frequent visitor, the lake offers something new and fascinating to offer.

New Experiences Await: From recently refurbished boutique hotels to enlarged hiking paths, Lake Garda is evolving. The region's tourist activities have increased access to its natural beauties while maintaining its charm.

Seasonal Festivals: In 2025, some of Lake Garda's most popular events will return, including the Bardolino Wine Festival and the Limone sul Garda Lemon Festival. These celebrations highlight the region's rich traditions and welcoming atmosphere.

Sustainability Focus: This year, Lake Garda is focussing on eco-friendly tourism, providing additional options for visitors to enjoy the lake responsibly. Sustainable choices include electric boat cruises, green hotels, and zero-waste marketplaces.

Postcard-worthy Scenery: Each season at Lake Garda has its own appeal, and 2025 is no exception. Imagine yourself wandering through flower-filled gardens in the spring, lazing on sunshine beaches in the summer, or sipping wine among golden vineyards in the autumn.

Lake Garda is more than simply a destination; it's a sensory experience that will inspire and revitalise you.

Best Time to Visit

The timing of your vacation to Lake Garda is determined by your interests and chosen speed. Each season has its own charms.

Spring (March to May): As the flowers blossom and the temperature rises, Lake Garda changes into a thriving paradise. This is an ideal season for outdoor activities such as hiking, cycling, and visiting towns before the summer hordes arrive.

Summer (June to August): The lake comes alive with activity as people rush to its beaches and watersports centres. It's the perfect time for boating, swimming, and attending vibrant festivals. However, book your lodgings early because this is the busiest time of year.

Autumn (September to November): Lake Garda's vineyards and olive groves are bathed in a golden glow, making it a perfect destination for food and wine enthusiasts. The colder temperature is also perfect for sightseeing and relaxing vacations.

Winter (December to February): Despite being quieter, Lake Garda keeps its beauty. In communities such as Lazise and Malcesine, visitors may enjoy cosy lakeside strolls, spa getaways, and charming Christmas markets.

Pro Tip: If you don't like crowds, avoid mid-August. This is when Italians have their summer vacations, and Lake Garda may get very crowded

Local Etiquette and Cultural Tips

Lake Garda residents are recognised for their kind and inviting demeanour, yet following their traditions can enhance your experience. Here are some techniques that will help you blend in seamlessly:

Greetings: Italians value a pleasant "Buongiorno" (Good morning) or "Buonasera" (Good evening). A smile and a courteous demeanour go a long way.

Dining Etiquette: Meals in Italy are intended to be enjoyed. Avoid speeding through courses, and always wait for the server to signal when to pay the bill—no one will bring it until you ask. Tipping is encouraged but not required; rounding up or leaving a few euros is customary.

Dress Code: While Lake Garda is casual, modesty is desired, particularly at religious areas such as churches. For dining out, dress smart-casual.

Driving in the Region: If you're hiring a car, keep in mind the tiny roads and the passionate driving of the locals. Respect parking regulations and keep in mind that many historic districts are only accessible by foot.

Environmental Awareness: Locals take pride in Lake Garda's pristine beauty. Help to preserve it by disposing of waste responsibly and using environmentally friendly transportation whenever possible.

By embracing the local culture, you will form stronger bonds and create lasting memories.

Lake Garda is a destination that entices visitors with its timeless appeal and numerous services. Whether you're drawn to the scenic shores, vibrant towns, or culinary delights, your trip to Lake Garda in 2025 will be unforgettable.

Getting To Lake Garda

With so many transportation options, planning your trip to Lake Garda can be overwhelming, but don't worry—it's easier than you think. Lake Garda is well-connected, making it easily accessible from major Italian towns and foreign locations. Whether you're flying, taking public transportation, or driving, this guide will help you get to this breathtaking location with ease and confidence.

Airports Near Lake Garda

Lake Garda's central position in northern Italy brings it near numerous international airports, providing vacationers lots of alternatives. Here's a summary of the main choices:

Verona Villafranca Airport (VRN) is the nearest airport, located about 15 kilometres (9 miles) from Lake Garda's southern shoreline. It's great for visitors visiting famous destinations like Peschiera del Garda, Bardolino, and Lazise. Taxis, car rentals, and shuttle buses make transfers seamless.

Bergamo Orio al Serio Airport (BGY): Located approximately 80 kilometres (50 miles) from Lake Garda's western shore, Bergamo Airport is a popular destination for budget-conscious travellers, with many low-cost airlines flying here. A combination of train and bus, or car rental, will take you to the lake in approximately 1.5 hours.

Milan Malpensa Airport (MXP) and Milan Linate Airport (LIN): Both Milan airports are approximately 120–140 kilometers (75–87 miles) from Lake Garda. They are excellent choices if you want to combine your Lake Garda trip with a visit to Milan.

Venice Marco Polo Airport (VCE): Situated around 130 kilometers (81 miles) from the eastern side of Lake Garda, Venice Airport is a great choice for travelers wanting to visit both Venice and the lake.

Tips for Airport Transfers
- To save time and avoid last-minute stress, schedule a transfer or rent a car ahead of time.
- Check for shuttle buses to important towns like Verona and Brescia, which are easily accessible from Lake Garda.

Train and Bus Connections

Italy's efficient train and bus systems make public transportation a stress-free and eco-friendly way to reach Lake Garda. Here's how to plan your trip:

By Train: Lake Garda is accessible via the Italian railway network, with stations conveniently located near the lake's key towns:
- Peschiera del Garda: Located on the southeastern coast, this station is great if you're headed to places like Lazise or Bardolino. It's served by high-speed trains from major cities like Milan, Venice, and Verona.
- Desenzano del Garda: On the southwestern shore, this station is a hub for exploring Sirmione and nearby attractions. It's also on the high-speed rail route, making travel speedy and pleasant.

Trains to these stations run frequently, and the journey times are short:
- From Verona: About 15–20 minutes
- From Milan: About 1–1.5 hours
- From Venice: About 1.5–2 hours

By Bus: Once you arrive at a nearby train station, buses will take you to the lakeside towns and attractions.
- Local Buses: Operated by firms like ATV (Verona region) and Arriva (Brescia region), these are dependable and inexpensive. Check schedules in advance, since services may be less frequent on weekends and holidays.
- Tourist Shuttle Buses: During peak season, some towns offer shuttle services specifically for visitors. These are a useful method to tour several regions without having a car.

Tips for Train and Bus Travel:
- Buy tickets online or at the station to save time.
- Validate your train or bus ticket before boarding to avoid a penalty. Look for the little validation devices at platforms or bus stops.
- Keep smaller money handy for local bus fares, as drivers may not accept large notes.

Driving to Lake Garda: Tips & Routes

For greatest flexibility, driving to Lake Garda is a wonderful alternative, especially if you want to tour numerous cities or drive into the surrounding countryside. The roads are well-maintained, and picturesque routes abound, but there are a few things to bear in mind.

Driving Routes to Lake Garda
- From Verona: Take the A4 highway (Autostrada Serenissima) toward Milan and leave at Peschiera del Garda or Desenzano del Garda, depending on your destination. The drive takes around 30-45 minutes.
- From Milan, take the A4 highway eastward towards Venice. Depending on your location, you can exit in Sirmione, Desenzano, or Peschiera. The trip takes roughly 1.5–2 hours.
- From Venice, take the A4 freeway west to Milan, then leave at Peschiera del Garda. The drive takes around 1.5 hours.

Parking in Lake Garda Towns
Parking might be difficult in some of the smaller towns, particularly during high seasons. Look for the alternatives below:
- Public Parking Lots: These are clearly designated and placed near town centres. Some charge a little fee, so bring cash or utilise a parking app if accessible.
- Hotel Parking: Many lodgings have private parking, which is frequently included in your

stay. Confirm this when you reserve your accommodation.

Driving Tips
- Toll Roads: Most Italian highways are toll roads. Keep cash or a credit card available at toll booths, or consider purchasing a Telepass for faster entry.
- ZTL Zones: Many ancient town centres are located in "Zona a Traffico Limitato" (ZTL) zones, which restrict inhabitants' car access. Pay heed to the signs to avoid penalties.
- Fuel: There are several petrol stations, however many are self-service and may demand cash or a card. If you want to have an attendant fill your tank, look for "Servito".
- Navigation: Use GPS or a trusted map program to prevent making erroneous turns, especially on tiny country roads.

Advantages of driving:
- Freedom to explore hidden jewels and less-accessible regions.
- Flexibility to make your own schedule and avoid relying on public transportation timings.

Challenges to Prepare For:
- Roads are narrow in certain regions, particularly near tiny communities.
- Parking is limited during busy tourist seasons.

Whatever method you choose to go to Lake Garda, you can be confident that with a little planning, your journey will be easy. Whether you prefer the convenience of trains, the affordability of buses, or the freedom of driving, travelling to Lake Garda is only the beginning of a memorable trip.

Where to Stay in Lake Garda

Finding the ideal spot to stay near Lake Garda is an exciting aspect of arranging your vacation. The region has a wide range of hotels, including family-friendly resorts, isolated romantic retreats, budget-friendly gems, and magnificent villas. Whether you're travelling with kids, your significant other, or looking for a lone getaway, you'll discover a place that feels just right. Let this guide assist you in making an educated decision, ensuring that your stay is as comfortable and pleasurable as the experiences that await you by the lake.

Best Areas for Families

Travelling with children? Lake Garda features several family-friendly locations that appeal to visitors of all ages.

Peschiera del Garda: Located on the southern shore, Peschiera is a popular family destination due to its closeness to Gardaland, Italy's largest amusement park. Many hotels and vacation parks in the vicinity include large rooms, children's groups, and swimming pools. The town's flat geography makes it simple to go around with strollers, and the seaside promenade is ideal for leisurely family hikes.

Bardolino: Known for its calm environment, Bardolino, has a mix of family-run hotels and vacation flats. The town has secure beaches with calm seas, which are great for young children. There are also plenty of gelaterias to keep youngsters (and adults) delighted.

Desenzano del Garda: This lively town on Lake Garda's southern shore offers family-friendly services as well as excellent transit links. It is an excellent base for day outings to neighbouring sites such as Parco Natura Viva, a zoo and safari park that children will love.

Tips for Families:
- Look for lodgings that include kitchenettes so you can easily make meals.
- Choose a location with on-site playgrounds or activities to keep youngsters occupied during downtime.

Romantic Escapes for Couples

Lake Garda is an ideal getaway for couples, with magnificent scenery, private cottages, and several romantic sites to share a moment.

Sirmione: Known as the "Pearl of Lake Garda," Sirmione is ideal for couples seeking a mix of romance and history. Stay at a boutique hotel overlooking the lake and see the old **Scaliger Castle** and **Catullus Grottoes** together. Don't miss Sirmione's famed thermal baths, which provide a luxurious experience for two.

Malcesine: Located on the lake's eastern bank, Malcesine is a picturesque village ideal for a romantic break. The picturesque cobblestone lanes, the imposing **Scaliger Castle**, and the scenic cable car journey to Monte Baldo make it a couple's dream. Many hotels here have private balconies with lake views, which are ideal for watching sunsets together.

Limone sul Garda: For a peaceful and private vacation, visit Limone. Nestled on the lake's northern side, this village boasts beautiful boutique hotels surrounded by lemon orchards and breathtaking views. Its serene atmosphere is great for couples seeking leisure.

Romantic Tip: Reserve a lakeside meal at one of the numerous restaurants that offer candlelight tables and views of the glistening water.

Budget-Friendly Accommodation

Travelling on a budget should not imply losing comfort or charm. Lake Garda has a variety of low-cost solutions that give great value.

Camping Villages: Lake Garda is filled with well-equipped camping towns that welcome families, couples, and lone travellers. Many of them have bungalows or mobile homes equipped with kitchens, as well as pools, restaurants, and recreational activities. Popular campsites include Camping Bella Italia near Peschiera and Camping Spiaggia D'Oro in Lazise.

Guesthouses and B&Bs: Small, family-run guesthouses and B&Bs are an excellent way to save money while still receiving a warm, personal touch. Towns like Desenzano and Torbole provide several economical choices for a comfortable stay without breaking the budget.

Affordable Hotels: Cheap hotels can be found in locations such as Riva del Garda and Garda Town. These frequently feature free breakfast and are placed within walking distance to major attractions.

Budget Tip: Travelling during the shoulder seasons (spring and fall) can allow you to discover reduced prices and enjoy the lake with less people.

Luxury Resorts and Villas

If you want a taste of wealth, Lake Garda has some of Italy's most expensive lodgings.

Grand Hotel Fasano (Gardone Riviera): This five-star hotel has exquisite accommodations, a world-class spa, and a luxurious lakefront location. Its verdant landscapes and exquisite dining options make it an ideal destination for those seeking luxury.

Villa Cortine Palace Hotel (Sirmione): Located on a private estate in Sirmione, this luxurious house boasts sumptuous apartments, tranquil gardens, and breathtaking views of the lake. It's ideal for individuals seeking seclusion and elegance.

Private Villas: For a truly luxurious vacation, rent a private villa. Many villas have infinity pools, personal cooks, and concierge services. Bardolino and Desenzano are popular villa rental destinations.

Luxury Tip: Many luxury establishments include special activities such as private boat trips or winery visits, which are ideal for enhancing your Lake Garda stay.

Sustainable Lodging Options

Lake Garda is home to a growing number of environmentally friendly lodgings.

Eco-Friendly Hotels: Properties such as Aqualux Hotel Spa & Suite Bardolino have been developed with sustainability in mind, including energy-efficient systems, environmentally friendly materials, and locally sourced dining alternatives.

Agriturismos: Staying on a farm is not only environmentally friendly, but it also provides a unique opportunity to engage with local customs. Many of these hotels, such as Agriturismo La Part, emphasise organic farming and serve home-cooked meals created with their own food.

Green Camping: Campgrounds like Camping Al Sole in Limone have implemented eco-friendly techniques such as solar electricity and recycling programs.

Sustainability Tip: Look for ISO 14001 or EcoLabel certificates to help support lodgings that prioritise environmental responsibility.

In conclusion, Lake Garda has a wide range of lodging alternatives to meet any traveler's needs, budget, and tastes. There are several excellent places to base yourself, ranging from family-friendly resorts and romantic retreats to eco-conscious hotels and luxury villas. Wherever you stay, you can expect to wake up to Lake Garda's magnificent beauty and wonderful experiences, making every moment of your holiday really memorable.

Must-See Attractions

Lake Garda is more than simply Italy's largest lake; it is a world of beauty, history, and charm that captivates every visitor. From mediaeval castles and romantic gardens to magnificent mountain panoramas and small towns, every aspect of this region whispers history while providing spectacular views. Here are five must-see sights that will leave you in amazement and nostalgia, making your Lake Garda experience unforgettable.

Scaliger Castle in Sirmione

Scaliger Castle, which rises impressively above the blue waters of Lake Garda, is reminiscent of a

fantasy. The Scaliger family built this fortification in the 13th century, and it is one of Italy's best-preserved fortresses. As you cross the drawbridge, you'll feel as if you've gone back in time to the days of knights and stories.

The castle's strategic location on the point of the Sirmione peninsula means it is surrounded by sea on three sides. Climb the castle's turrets to see panoramic views of the glistening lake, Sirmione's terracotta roofs, and the surrounding Alps. Inside, explore the cobblestone courtyards and envision the life of individuals who formerly passed through these old hallways.

For a truly magnificent experience, go around sunset, when the golden light bathes the castle and lake, creating an almost mythological ambiance.

Vittoriale degli Italiani in Gardone Riviera

The Vittoriale degli Italiani, perched on Lake Garda's western coast, is more than simply a palace; it's a masterwork of eccentricity and patriotism. Gabriele D'Annunzio, a well-known poet, soldier, and aviator, previously lived on this enormous estate. Today, it serves as a tribute to his outsized personality and Italy's cultural history.

As you explore through its luxurious halls, you'll come across artefacts from D'Annunzio's colourful life, including elaborate furnishings, enormous libraries, and odd curiosities. Step outdoors into the wide gardens, where you'll discover surprises around every corner—a ship embedded in the hillside, an open-air amphitheatre with panoramic views of the lake, and fountains that bring a touch of peace to this diverse wonderland.

The Vittoriale degli Italiani is more than just a museum; it's an excursion into the psyche of one of Italy's most intriguing historical people. The mix of art, history, and natural beauty makes it a must-see visit on any Lake Garda itinerary.

Monte Baldo's Panoramic Views

Monte Baldo is a must-see site for people seeking adventure and breathtaking views. Known as the

"Garden of Europe," this tall peak provides some of the most spectacular views of Lake Garda and its surroundings.

Begin your tour at Malcesine, where the cable car transports you to Monte Baldo's peak. The trip itself is thrilling, with revolving cabins offering a 360-degree view of the lake, verdant valleys, and rocky peaks of the Italian Alps. When you reach the top, you are welcomed by a breathtaking panorama that feels almost dreamlike.

Take a leisurely walk along the mountain pathways, where alpine vegetation blooms in the warmer months. In the winter, Monte Baldo changes into a snowy wonderland that draws skiers and snowboarders. Monte Baldo will leave you in wonder, whether you come for a morning walk, a picnic with a view or simply to take in the fresh mountain air.

The Charming Streets of Malcesine

Malcesine feels like it was stolen from a storybook. This charming village on the lake's eastern bank is a

tangle of cobblestone lanes, pastel-colored cottages, and bougainvillea-draped balconies.

The Scaliger Castle, another Lake Garda beauty, is located in the centre of Malcesine. While not as big as its cousin in Sirmione, it retains a certain charm. Climb the tower for breathtaking views of the lake and Monte Baldo, and then visit the castle's tiny museum to learn about the area's history and natural beauty.

Walking through Malcesine is a pleasure in itself. Discover artisan stores selling handcrafted items, cosy cafés where you can sip espresso by the river, and secret lanes that lead to peaceful courtyards. As you stroll, the serene presence of the lake is constantly around, making Malcesine a town that begs you to slow down and enjoy the moment.

Limone sul Garda's Lemon Groves

The name "Limone sul Garda" may imply a relationship to lemons, and this lovely community surely lives up to that moniker. Limone, located on the lake's northern side, is known for its terraced lemon orchards, which have been farmed since the 13th century.

Take a leisurely tour around the Limonaia del Castel, a beautifully preserved lemon home where you can learn about local citrus farming history. The aroma of lemons permeates the air as you walk across the terraces, which give views of the lake bordered by lush flora.

Limone's splendour does not stop with its groves. The hamlet itself is a treat to explore, with its small streets, vibrant shops, and seaside cafés. Try local lemon-based specialities such as limoncello and delicious lemon sorbet. Limone is a must-see destination for anybody visiting Lake Garda because of its natural beauty, history, and cuisine.

In conclusion, each of these must-see sights provides a distinct perspective on the beauty and history of Lake Garda. From the mediaeval grandeur of Scaliger Castle to the beautiful gardens of Vittoriale, the sweeping vistas of Monte Baldo, the charm of Malcesine, and the fragrant lemon orchards of Limone, these sites encapsulate the spirit of this magical area.

Whether you're drawn to Lake Garda by history, natural wonders, or the simple delight of meandering through gorgeous neighbourhoods, you'll have memories that will last a lifetime. As you visit these historic locations, you'll not only see the region's beauty, but also experience a strong connection to its soul—a timeless attraction that has inspired numerous travellers throughout history.

Hidden Gems of Lake Garda

While Lake Garda's major attractions and magnificent landscape captivate visitors, it is the hidden jewels that truly capture the spirit of adventure and discovery. Beyond the iconic sites, there are hidden treasures waiting to be discovered, each with its own distinct narrative and attraction. These off-the-beaten-path sites provide a more personal connection to the region, ideal for travellers looking to go beyond the conventional. Here are four wonderful hidden jewels that will pique your interest and astonishment.

Borghetto sul Mincio: A Picturesque Riverside Hamlet

Borghetto sul Mincio, located along the Mincio River, is reminiscent of a Renaissance picture. This little village, which is sometimes overlooked by the busy towns of Lake Garda, is a sanctuary of peace and timeless beauty. Cobbled lanes twist between historic stone houses covered with climbing vines and flower-filled balconies, while the gentle sound of water flowing from the river adds to the tranquil atmosphere.

The Ponte Visconteo, a mediaeval dam bridge erected in the 14th century, is the village's most visible landmark. Walking across this old structure, with its breathtaking views of the surrounding countryside, seems like going back in time.

Stop by a nearby trattoria to have tortellini di Valeggio, a delicate pasta dish unique to the area. As you dine al fresco, the calm pace of life in Borghetto begs you to stay and enjoy the charm of this riverbank jewel. For the daring, cycling along the Mincio River bike route is an excellent opportunity to explore the area further.

Grotte di Catullo: Ancient Roman Ruins

Perched on the point of the Sirmione peninsula, the Grotte di Catullo provides an intriguing peek into the past. These old Roman remains, originally the location of a great villa, demonstrate the region's rich history and architectural brilliance. Despite its name ("Grotte" translates to "caves"), this attraction is everything from underground. Instead, it's a huge structure of stone arches, walls, and terraces that overlook the glistening waters of Lake Garda.

As you meander around the remains, you can easily envision the lavish lifestyle of the Roman aristocracy who once resided here. The estate offered breathtaking vistas, hot spas, and even its own olive grove. Today, the olive trees thrive, contributing to the area's rustic appeal.

The neighbouring museum gives useful context for the villa and the artefacts recovered here, ranging from mosaics to ceramics. But the true charm is found in visiting the site itself, where whispers of history combine with the calm air from the lake. Visit early in the morning or late in the afternoon to see the remains drenched in golden light—an incredible sight.

Isola del Garda: A Private Island Retreat

Imagine a verdant island filled with exotic gardens and topped with a Venetian-style palace. Isola del Garda is Lake Garda's biggest island and a hidden beauty that feels like a planet away from the mainland. Although the island is privately owned, guided visits provide a unique opportunity to appreciate its beauty.

Arriving by boat, you'll be met by the sight of Villa Cavazza, a beautiful 19th-century home that rises like a diamond from the island's lush foliage. The guided tour leads you through the villa's vast rooms, which are adorned with period furnishings, art, and history. But it's the gardens that really steal the show. Winding trails take you past scented citrus trees, colourful blossoms, and stunning views of the lake.

The island's tranquility and exclusivity make it an ideal destination for both nature enthusiasts and history historians. It's also an excellent location for photography, with stunning views around every curve. If you're seeking a memorable retreat, Isola del Garda offers an experience that is both spectacular and very intimate.

Sanctuary of Madonna della Corona: A Cliffside Marvel

For those looking for spiritual inspiration or just a breathtaking vista, the Sanctuary of Madonna della Corona is a must-see hidden gem. This hallowed structure, which clings steeply to the face of Monte Baldo, is both an architectural wonder and a haven of deep peace.

To get to the sanctuary, trek up a picturesque route from the town of Brentino, which rewards you with spectacular views of the Adige valley. For a more relaxing approach, Spiazzi's shuttle service can transport you closer to the location.

As you approach, the sanctuary appears to spring smoothly from the rock—a miracle of engineering and faith. Inside, the church is decorated with stunning paintings, votive offerings, and a peaceful solemnity.

Step outdoors onto the terraces to enjoy breathtaking views of the valley below. Whether you come for prayer, reflection, or to simply admire its beauty, the Sanctuary of Madonna della Corona is a testament to human ingenuity and devotion.

In conclusion, aside from its famous attractions, Lake Garda's hidden gems offer a world of discovery. From the storybook charm of Borghetto sul Mincio and the ancient allure of the Grotte di Catullo to the serene elegance of Isola del Garda and the spiritual majesty of the Sanctuary of Madonna della Corona, these destinations invite you to see the lake in a whole new light.

Each of these locations serves as a reminder that Lake Garda is more than simply a place to visit; it is a place to explore, with every corner telling a tale and every discovery seeming like your own little secret. Whether you're drawn to Lake Garda by history, environment, or the promise of adventure, these hidden jewels will keep you captivated and delighted throughout your visit.

Fun Things to Do Around Lake Garda

Lake Garda is a playground for thrill seekers, relaxation enthusiasts, and everyone in between. Whether you are drawn to the lure of the vast outdoors, the glistening waterways, or the tempting flavours of the region, there is something to make your vacation memorable. From exhilarating activities to enlightening encounters, the excitement never stops. Let's have a look at some of the greatest things to do in and around this stunning Italian jewel.

Hiking and Cycling Trails

If you enjoy gorgeous experiences, Lake Garda's hiking and cycling routes will leave you feeling inspired. The region has a plethora of routes going through lush forests, undulating hills, and dramatic cliffs, with panoramic lake views as a constant companion.

Sentiero del Ponale is a popular trail among hikers. This classic route connects Riva del Garda to Lake Ledro, weaving among rocky outcrops and providing breathtaking views of the lake below. The well-maintained trail is appropriate for all ability levels, so whether you're a seasoned trekker or a casual walker, you'll feel energised and gratified by the adventure.

Cyclists will discover a variety of exciting routes, ranging from peaceful lakeside rides to tough ascents. The ***Garda by Bike*** initiative is a must-see—a breathtaking riding path that hugs the cliffs, giving the impression of hovering above the sea. Don't forget your camera since each bend exposes a postcard-perfect panorama.

Sailing and Water Sports

Lake Garda isn't only for admiring from the beach; its crystal-clear waters invite you to delve into a world of aquatic delights. Sailing fans travel to the lake because of its consistent winds, making it one of Europe's top locations for this activity. Whether you're an expert sailor or a beginner, you may hire a boat or join a guided tour to experience the excitement of skimming across the waves.

Windsurfing or kitesurfing in northern cities like Torbole and Malcesine offers a faster-paced excitement. If you want a more calm experience, paddleboarding or kayaking allows you to explore the lake at your own speed, taking in the tranquility of hidden coves and secluded inlets.

Banana boat rides and jet skiing are popular among adventurous families, while those looking for a one-of-a-kind experience may prefer a sunset cruise—watching the sun sink below the horizon as the lake reflects its golden colours is nothing short of breathtaking.

Hot Air Balloon Rides Over Lake Garda

Take to the sky in a hot air balloon to get a unique view of Lake Garda. Floating softly over the sea, you'll be treated to a breathtaking view of glittering blue waves, beautiful vineyards, and quaint villages tucked at the foot of the mountains.

This once-in-a-lifetime event is ideal for early risers, since the balloons often lift off around daybreak. As you rise, the world below becomes a tapestry of nature and history, and the serenity of the early air adds to the tranquility of the trip.

Some flights even include a post-ride toast with a glass of Prosecco, allowing you to enjoy your flying experience the Italian way. Whether you're travelling with a boyfriend, friends, or family, a hot air balloon flight over Lake Garda will undoubtedly be the highlight of your trip.

Wine Tasting in Bardolino

Italy and wine are inextricably linked, and Lake Garda's wine area is a wine lover's dream. Among the numerous lovely towns, Bardolino distinguishes it as the hub of the region's wine industry. Bardolino, known for its light and fruity red wines, encourages you to savour and immerse yourself in the region's flavours.

Begin your adventure at one of the numerous family-owned vineyards, where you'll be greeted and escorted through the winemaking process. From vineyard visits to tastings, you'll develop a profound appreciation for the craftsmanship behind each bottle. Don't miss out on trying the area's characteristic rosé, Bardolino Classico and Chiaretto, which has subtle floral and cherry aromas.

For a more in-depth experience, attend the Bardolino Wine Festival, which takes place every autumn. The town transforms into a wine-themed party, complete with tastings, live music, and a bustling ambiance as enticing as the beverages themselves.

Cooking Classes with Local Chefs

If you've ever wanted to learn Italian cuisine, Lake Garda provides the ideal chance. Sign up for a cooking lesson with a local chef and learn how to replicate the flavours of this fascinating region in your own kitchen.

Classes are sometimes held in scenic locations, such as rural farmhouses or villas overlooking the lake, which adds to the allure of the experience. You'll learn how to make fresh pasta, risotto, and real pizza while being guided by devoted chefs. Some seminars also teach how to make excellent sweets such as tiramisu and panna cotta.

What is the best part? You'll be able to enjoy the results of your labour in a friendly setting, accompanied with a glass of local wine. Not only will you depart with a full stomach and a contented heart, but you'll also take home recipes and abilities to keep the flavour of Lake Garda alive long after your holiday is over.

In conclusion, Lake Garda is a refuge for fun and adventure, with a wide range of activities to suit every interest. Whether you're hiking gorgeous paths, boating over sparkling waterways, flying above the lake in a hot air balloon, sampling local wines, or learning to prepare Italian cuisine, each activity offers amazing experiences.

This region is more than simply a destination; it's a location where every minute is full of possibilities. Lace up your hiking boots, grab your paddle and raise a glass—your Lake Garda experience awaits!

Dining & Local Cuisine in Lake Garda

Food is important to Italian culture, and Lake Garda provides an unparalleled gastronomic experience. From savoury traditional foods to sumptuous sweets, each taste here reflects the region's rich history and abundant natural resources. Dining at Lake Garda is a memorable experience, whether you're enjoying a candlelight supper by the water or discovering artisanal treasures like olive oil and wine.

Traditional Dishes of Lake Garda

Lake Garda cuisine is a delicious combination of northern Italian flavours and Mediterranean influences, based on local products and time-honoured techniques. Here are some must-try foods that will transport your taste buds:

- **Bigoli con le Sarde:** A regional speciality, this substantial pasta dish combines thick, spaghetti-like noodles with fresh lake sardines, garlic and parsley.
- **Risotto all'Amarone:** Made with Amarone wine, this delicious risotto has a velvety texture and a rich, somewhat sweet flavour.

- **Polenta e Coniglio:** A soothing meal of creamy polenta served with soft braised rabbit, which is frequently prepared with aromatic herbs and a splash of white wine.
- **Tortellini di Valeggio:** Known as "love knots," these delicate, hand-crafted pasta packages are stuffed with a variety of meats and spices and served with sage butter or broth.
- **Grilled Lavarello:** Also known as whitefish, this lake delicacy is traditionally grilled with olive oil and lemon to highlight its delicate flavour.

Best Lakefront Restaurants

Dining by the water is an important Lake Garda experience. Imagine yourself sipping a glass of wine while staring out at the glistening lake—a feast for both your taste and your eyes. Here are some noteworthy waterfront restaurants:

La Speranzina (Sirmione): This exquisite restaurant nestled in the Sirmione peninsula serves gourmet food while offering spectacular lake views. Try their unique seafood delicacies, such as octopus carpaccio and lobster ravioli.

Ristorante Al Boifava (Peschiera del Garda): This relaxing restaurant is ideal for families and foodies alike, with classic Italian cooking ranging from wood-fired pizzas to seasonal risottos.

La Torre di San Martino (Desenzano del Garda): Located beside a mediaeval tower, this quaint café provides classic meals with a modern touch, while offering magnificent views of the lake and hills.

Regio Patio (Gargnano): Regio Patio, a Michelin-starred restaurant, provides a sophisticated culinary experience with meals that include local delicacies such as freshwater fish and Garda lemons.

La Casa degli Spiriti (Costermano): For a romantic evening, this charming villa restaurant provides exceptional service, exquisite cuisine, and a stunning patio with panoramic views.

Exploring Olive Oil and Wine Tastings

Lake Garda is not just a foodie's dream, but also a refuge for wine and olive oil enthusiasts. The region is renowned for its excellent olive trees and vineyards, which provide flavours as distinct as the lake itself.

Olive Oil

- Visit the **Olive Oil Museum in Cisano** to learn about the history and manufacture of Garda's famous extra virgin olive oil.
- Arrange a taste at a local producer, such as **Frantoio Montecroce** in Desenzano, where you may sample oils ranging from fruity to peppery, all suitable for spreading over fresh bread or salads.
- Garda DOP olive oil is a must-have keepsake; its smooth, subtle flavour is valued across Italy.

Wine

- The Bardolino and Valpolicella areas are ideal for wine tasting.
- Look for **Chiaretto Rosé**, a light and aromatic wine that goes great with the lake's fresh fish.
- Visit a family-run winery like **Guerrieri Rizzardi**, where you can walk around the vines, learn about winemaking, and have a guided tasting.
- Don't miss **Lugana**, a crisp white wine developed on the lake's southern beaches that pairs well with fish meals.

Sweets: Gelato and More

No vacation to Italy is complete without sampling its world-renowned sweets, and Lake Garda is no exception. Here's what will satisfy your sweet tooth:

Gelato: Wander through lovely villages like Malcesine or Lazise, where handmade gelaterias entice with colourful displays of creamy treats. Gelateria Al Porto in Garda and Gelateria Caffè Cristallo in Sirmione are two popular places. Don't leave without sampling the pistachio, limone (lemon), and Amarena cherry flavours.

Torta della Nonna: This Italian custard pastry, topped with pine nuts and powdered sugar, is as soothing as a warm hug.

Sfogliatine di Villafranca: These delicate puff pastries, softly sweetened, are ideal for serving with coffee or tea.

Garda Lemons, known for their rich flavour, are frequently used to produce zesty sweets like lemon sorbet, tartlets, and Limoncello, a pleasant after-dinner liqueur.

Pandoro: Although usually linked with Verona, this buttery, star-shaped cake is a festive favourite near Lake Garda, particularly during the Christmas season.

A Culinary Adventure awaits
Lake Garda's food ranges from substantial pastas to delicate desserts, making it a sensory feast. Whether you're enjoying a lakeside supper, sampling the fruits of the region's vineyards and olive groves, or indulging in a creamy gelato while strolling along the beach, every eating experience here is steeped with warmth, passion, and the flavours of la dolce vita.

So take up a chair, pour yourself a glass of Chiaretto, and let Lake Garda's gastronomic enchantment enchant you. Good appetite!

Shopping in Lake Garda

Shopping at Lake Garda is as active and diversified as the surroundings. From lively local markets to artisan stores packed with homemade treasures and even opulent brand outlets, there's something for every type of shopper. Lake Garda offers an exceptional shopping experience, whether you're looking for one-of-a-kind mementos or treating yourself to a trendy splurge.

Markets in Lake Garda's Towns

Nothing better exemplifies Italian culture than its marketplaces. These vibrant centres are more than simply shopping destinations; they are communal meetings where both residents and visitors can appreciate the region's flavours, crafts, and customs.

Sirmione Market (Monday mornings): Located in the picturesque old town, this market sells everything from fresh food and cheeses to handcrafted jewellery and leather products. Wander the vendors and try local specialities like Garda olives and freshly baked foccaccia.

Bardolino Market (Thursday mornings): Located near the shore, this market offers a variety of regional cuisine, artisan goods, and trendy apparel. Its picturesque setting makes it a delight to explore.

Desenzano del Garda Market (Tuesday mornings): One of the area's largest markets, this lively event sells a variety of things such as gourmet foods, pottery, and home furnishings.

Riva del Garda Market (2nd and 4th Wednesdays of the month): Situated in the gorgeous northern portion of the lake, this market is ideal for purchasing regional wines, organic vegetables, and handmade textiles.

Insider Tip: Arrive early for the greatest choices, and bring cash as not all vendors take credit cards.

Artisan Crafts and Souvenirs

For visitors looking for one-of-a-kind souvenirs, Lake Garda's artisan boutiques and workshops are a dream come true. The region's crafts reflect its rich tradition and natural beauty, making each piece a valuable keepsake.

Handmade Ceramics: Ceramiche La Felice in Peschiera del Garda offers hand-painted ceramics with themes inspired by the lake's surroundings. These pieces, ranging from plates to ornamental tiles, are exquisite presents.

Olive Wood Products: The plentiful olive trees surrounding the lake supply material for beautiful hand-carved handicrafts. Look for bowls, chopping boards, and cutlery at stores such as ArteLegno in Lazise.

Jewellery & Accessories: In Sirmione and Malcesine, artisans produce beautiful items out of Murano glass beads and semi-precious stones, ideal for adding a bit of Italian flare to your outfit.

Limoncello & Local Delicacies: Take home a taste of Lake Garda with bottles of limoncello, Garda DOP olive oil, or citrus marmalade. Many small businesses in Bardolino and Torri del Benaco provide wine gift boxes including Chiaretto or Lugana.

Textiles & Lace: In places like Garda and Valeggio sul Mincio, you may get handcrafted lace and embroidered linen. These exquisite pieces are great for bringing a touch of Italian flair to any room.

Designer Outlets Near The Lake

For a splash of glam, visit the designer stores around Lake Garda, where you can get high-end clothing and accessories at discounted costs. These shopping sites appeal to fashion fans searching for high-end products without breaking the budget.

Franciacorta Outlet Village: This outlet, located about an hour from the lake, is a fashion lover's delight. With over 160 retailers, including Gucci, Versace, and Michael Kors, it's the ideal place to update your wardrobe. Enjoy the attractively constructed open-air layout and several food alternatives for a well-rounded shopping experience.

Mantova Outlet Village: Located southeast of the lake, this lovely outlet has a mix of worldwide names like Nike and Calvin Klein, as well as Italian mainstays like Furla and Twinset. The savings are appealing, and the casual environment makes it a nice outing.

Fidenza Village: A bit further away but well worth the drive, this opulent outlet has major brands such as Prada, Armani, and Salvatore Ferragamo. The village-like atmosphere and VIP services enhance the shopping experience.

Pro Tip: Many stores provide additional savings during seasonal sales or for tourists, so make sure to check the visitor information centres for specials and promotions.

In summary, Shopping at Lake Garda is more than simply a transaction; it's an expression of the area's culture, creativity, and flair. Whether you're meandering through bustling markets, discovering the beauty behind local crafts, or indulging in a luxury shopping spree, each encounter is imbued with the spirit of Italian la dolce vita.

So take your shopping bags and enter the vivid world of Lake Garda's retail treasures—you'll be sure to depart with not just one-of-a-kind purchases but also fond memories of your experience.

Family-Friendly Fun at Lake Garda

Lake Garda is a fascinating place that offers thrills and adventures for people of all ages. Whether you're riding roller coasters, witnessing animals, splashing at family-friendly beaches, or on a boat cruise, every moment is filled with excitement and laughter. The kids will be overjoyed, while the parents will enjoy the combination of leisure and excitement. Let's dig into the family-friendly activities available in Lake Garda!

Gardaland Theme Park: A World of Wonders

Welcome to Gardaland, where creativity meets excitement! This world-renowned theme park in Castelnuovo del Garda offers rides, shows, and activities for all members of the family.

Thrills for All Ages: Children will love Peppa Pig Land, which features pint-sized rides and meet-and-greet chances. Heart-pounding roller coasters like the Raptor and Blue Tornado provide high-speed exhilaration for older children (and their daring parents).

Fantasy Kingdom: Enter a fanciful world where magic comes to life. The brightly coloured carousel, treehouse excursions, and live performances will transport the entire family to a fairytale setting.

Interactive Shows: Enjoy stunning presentations with acrobatics, music, and even 4D movie experiences that immerse you in imaginative stories.

Top Tip: Buy your tickets online to avoid the lines, and add the Gardaland SEA LIFE Aquarium to your itinerary for an underwater adventure.

Parco Natura Viva: A Safari Adventure

Parco Natura Viva, a wildlife sanctuary just a short drive from the lake, is ideal for animal lovers. This huge park mixes a safari experience with a classic zoo, keeping your little explorers enthralled from beginning to end.

Safari Park: Drive around the safari region and see gorgeous animals like lions, zebras, and rhinos living freely in their natural habitats. The thrill of seeing these animals up close is incomparable!

Walking Trails: Explore the fauna park, where you may see creatures such as red pandas, meerkats, and flamingos. Each cage is meant to imitate the creatures' natural surroundings, making the experience both instructive and enjoyable.

Dino Park: The park's dinosaur section is a favourite with children, with life-sized representations of prehistoric species. Allow the youngsters to envision themselves as junior palaeontologists on an exciting Jurassic journey!

Insider Tip: Bring comfortable shoes, food, and lots of water for your visit, and don't forget your camera to record the kids' responses to the animals.

Boat Trips with Kids: Adventure on the Water

Exploring Lake Garda by boat is a must-do experience that the entire family will enjoy. These boat cruises, with their glistening waterways, stunning sights, and sense of adventure, are ideal for making lasting memories.

Ferry Rides: Board a public ferry and travel between picturesque towns like Sirmione, Malcesine, and Limone sul Garda. The leisurely pace and open-air decks offer a delightful way to explore the lake.

Private Boat Tours: For a more personalised experience, charter a private boat and plan your own route. Many operators provide family-friendly itineraries that include pauses for swimming and exploring secret coves.

Pirate-Themed Cruises: Some operators provide themed boat cruises that are popular with children. Imagine sailing the high seas (or the lake) on a pirate ship, complete with eye coverings!

Safety First: Life jackets are usually given, but it's always a good idea to check with the operator. Bring sunscreen, hats, and snacks to ensure everyone's comfort.

Top Beaches for Families

Lake Garda's beaches are more than simply beautiful; they're a refuge for families looking for sun, sand, and plenty of fun. Here are some of the greatest places for parents to relax while their children play around and create sandcastles.

Spiaggia Sabbioni (Riva del Garda): This expansive beach has everything a family could possibly need, including covered picnic spaces, a playground, and quiet, shallow waves. The grassy spaces are ideal for relaxing while the children enjoy the water.

Lido di Lazise: Located near the village of Lazise, this sandy beach is ideal for families. With neighbouring cafés, ice cream stalls, and lots of room to sprawl out, it's an excellent choice for a day of fun in the sun.

Baia delle Sirene (Punta San Vigilio): Known for its crystal-clear waters and peaceful location, this beach is great for families seeking relaxation and scenic beauty. Shaded spaces under olive trees offer shelter from the sun.

Pisenze Beach (Manerba del Garda): This pebbled beach has shallow waters suitable for little swimmers. Bring water shoes for comfort, and relax in the calm surroundings.

Pro Tip: Arrive early to get a nice location, especially during the peak summer season. Don't forget beach toys and floaties for more enjoyment!

In conclusion, Lake Garda is more than simply a vacation; it is an infinite playground for families.

From exhilarating roller coasters at Gardaland to calm boat excursions and animal encounters at Parco Natura Viva, the area provides an ideal balance of adrenaline and relaxation. When you combine the sun-dappled beaches with the thrill of exploring together, you have the ideal recipe for family bonding.

Pack your sense of wonder and prepare to create memories that will last long after your Lake Garda holiday ends. After all, the finest trips are shared with the people you care about the most!

Romantic Experiences at Lake Garda

Lake Garda has a way of creating charm in every nook, making it an ideal scene for romance. With its glistening waves, charming towns, and romantic sunsets, this wonderful place welcomes couples to celebrate love in all its forms. Whether you're wandering hand in hand through picturesque towns, relaxing in a spa, or having a private picnic under an olive tree canopy, Lake Garda provides personal moments that seem like they belong in a romance story. Let's look at some of the most pleasant moments for couples at this gorgeous Italian retreat.

Sunset Cruises on Lake Garda

Few things are more compelling than watching the sun go below the horizon from the middle of Lake Garda. A sunset cruise is the pinnacle of romance, enveloping you and your sweetheart in the lake's golden glow as you sail across its tranquil waters.

- **Private Boat Tours:** For a unique experience, charter a private boat and sail into the evening. Toast your love with a glass of Prosecco while the beautiful light

illuminates the surrounding hills and villages.
- **Group Sunset Cruises:** Join a group cruise for a fun but intimate setting. Many cruises provide live music, aperitifs, and even candlelight dinners on board.
- **Magical Views:** As the day fades, the lake's beauty transforms—its waters sparkle with amber, pink, and violet hues, resulting in an ever-changing masterpiece.

Pro Tip: Bring a light shawl or jacket to remain warm as the temperature drops after dusk. Most cruises leave from Sirmione, Bardolino, or Garda town, so plan to arrive early and visit these wonderful towns first.

Couples' Spa Retreats

Rejuvenate your body and spirit at one of Lake Garda's luxury spas, where thermal waters, delicious treatments, and tranquil settings create a haven of peace.

- **Terme di Sirmione:** This world-famous spa, located on the lake's southern point, is a romantic retreat. Soak in the restorative thermal baths, have a couples massage, or

relax in the lakeside thermal pools with panoramic views.
- **Aqualux Hotel Spa & Suite (Bardolino):** This eco-luxury resort provides bespoke wellness packages for couples, including aromatherapy and deep-tissue massages. The serene grounds and stylish setting contribute to the romantic attraction.
- **Intimate Touches:** Many spas provide unique experiences such as private thermal pools, romantic massages, and rooftop hot tubs under the stars.

Pro Tip: Schedule your treatments in advance, especially during weekends or high seasons, to ensure that you and your spouse receive the pampering you deserve.

Hidden Picnic Spots

Imagine having a picnic surrounded by olive orchards, vineyards, or rolling hills, with the peaceful sounds of the lake in the background. Lake Garda is overflowing with hidden locations ideal for a romantic outdoor supper.

- **Punta San Vigilio:** This lovely peninsula has postcard-perfect vistas and peaceful

areas for a relaxing picnic. Combine a basket of local cheese, fresh bread, and Bardolino wine with the tranquil beauty of this hidden gem.
- **Monte Baldo:** After a spectacular cable car journey, seek out a private area on the verdant slopes of Monte Baldo. The amazing panoramic vistas enhance the flavour of each mouthful.
- **Isola del Garda:** If you want to experience something genuinely unusual, consider visiting this private island. Some visits include picnics in the island's beautiful gardens, which are surrounded by exotic flora and old structures.

Pack the Essentials: Visit local markets for picnic goods such as fresh fruit, cured meats, and homemade pastries. Don't forget to pack a blanket and possibly a love note in your basket.

Romantic Villages to Explore

The lovely villages surrounding Lake Garda appear to have been constructed specifically for lovers. With cobblestone alleys, flower-filled balconies, and peaceful waterfronts, these gorgeous locations beg you to slow down and enjoy every minute together.

Sirmione: Sirmione, also known as the "Pearl of the Lake," is a romantic haven with its mediaeval alleyways, the renowned Scaliger Castle, and the relaxing charm of its lakeside promenade. Don't miss out on seeing the Grotte di Catullo, which combines history with breathtaking vistas.

Malcesine: Perched at the foot of Monte Baldo, this charming town enchants visitors with its pastel-colored homes, small alleyways, and majestic Scaliger Castle. Climb the castle's tower for breathtaking lake views—the ideal location for a snapshot with your lover.

Limone sul Garda: Known for its lemon gardens, this community emanates old-world charm. Wander through its peaceful streets together, then toast with limoncello as the sun sets.

Torbole: For couples who enjoy nature, this community offers peaceful walks and beachfront eating. It's a less crowded option that nevertheless offers plenty of romance.

In summary, Lake Garda is more than simply a vacation; it's a backdrop for love stories. Whether you're floating over the lake on a sunset cruise, basking in spa bliss, exploring hidden picnic sites, or immersing yourself in the beauty of romantic towns, each encounter seems like it's meant to bring you together.

Time slows down here, and simple moments—a shared chuckle, a lingering stare, a toast to the future—become unforgettable. So grab your partner's hand, let the charm of Lake Garda envelop you, and make memories that will last long after you return home.

Outdoor Adventures on Lake Garda

If your ideal holiday includes adrenaline-pumping sports and immersion in nature's raw beauty, Lake Garda is the place for you. From conquering steep cliffs to flying over turquoise lakes and seeing beautiful parks, this place offers excitement at every step. Its diverse topography, crystal-clear lake, and temperate temperature make it a dream destination for adventure seekers and outdoor enthusiasts alike. Here's your guide to some of the most thrilling outdoor excursions near Lake Garda.

Canyoning and Rock Climbing

Experience the excitement of negotiating Lake Garda's rugged gorges and climbing its beautiful cliffs. Canyoning and rock climbing are must-do sports for anybody wishing to push themselves while admiring the region's breathtaking natural splendour.

Canyoning Adventures: Canyoning adventures include following the route of mountain streams, abseiling down waterfalls, sliding through natural rock chutes, and wading through crystal clear pools. Popular spots include Vione Canyon and Palvico

Canyon, where skilled guides will guarantee your journey is both safe and memorable.

Rock Climbing Hotspots: The northern portion of Lake Garda, especially around Arco, is a climber's paradise. Climbers from all over the world flock to this location because of its limestone cliffs and routes for all ability levels. Whether you're an experienced climber or a beginner, Arco has a route for you.

Gear Up: Don't be concerned about equipment; most canyoning and climbing programs provide all essential gear and skilled coaching. Simply bring your daring spirit!

Pro Tip: Book excursions early in the morning to take advantage of milder temperatures and calmer trails, allowing you to make the most of your trip.

Paragliding Over Lake Garda

Enjoy the ultimate freedom as you fly through the air, taking in the spectacular views of Lake Garda and its surrounding mountains. Paragliding provides a unique view of this gorgeous location, leaving you feeling awestruck and exhilarated.

Take off from Monte Baldo: Monte Baldo is the preferred location for paragliding over Lake Garda. Its high peaks and mild thermals make an ideal launchpad for flying over the sky. The descent provides panoramic views of the lake, charming villages, and lush countryside.

Tandem Flights for Beginners: No prior experience? Not a problem! Tandem flights with skilled pilots allow you to experience the excitement of paragliding without prior training. All you need to do is sit back and enjoy the journey.

Best Time to Fly: Paragliding is best done in the morning or late afternoon when the air is calm and the light creates a wonderful glow across the countryside.

Capture the Moment: Many paragliding trips provide GoPro film, allowing you to relive and share your flight with friends and family.

Exploring Alto Garda Bresciano Park

Escape to the wildness of Alto Garda Bresciano Park, a vast natural reserve with limitless chances for outdoor adventure. This park is ideal for hikers, cyclists, and wildlife enthusiasts looking to see the wild side of Lake Garda.

Hiking Trails: Choose from a network of paths that range from short strolls to strenuous hikes. The *Sentiero delle Trincee* (Trenches Trail) connects ancient places with beautiful vistas, while the *Toscolano-Maderno* Path leads through lush forests and past tumbling waterfalls.

Mountain Biking: Bring your own bike or hire one locally to take on thrilling trails such as the *Garda Panorama Trail*. The combination of challenging climbs and exciting descents will keep your adrenaline flowing.

Flora & Fauna: Keep a watch out for natural animals such as deer, foxes, and other bird species. In the spring, the park is alive with wildflowers, producing beautiful arrays of colour.

Tips for a Day in the Park: Bring a picnic, lots of water, and sturdy footwear. Many routes feature lovely rest places where you may take a break and appreciate the natural beauty around you.

Kayaking and Paddleboarding

The calm, clear waters of Lake Garda make an ideal location for kayaking and paddleboarding. These activities allow you to engage with the lake in a more intimate way, combining adventure and relaxation.

Why Kayaking? Glide through secret coves, see isolated beaches, and get unique views of lakeside towns like Sirmione and Malcesine. Many rental businesses provide guided trips that mix paddling and sightseeing.

Stand-Up Paddleboarding (SUP) has grown in popularity due to its ability to provide both leisure and exercise. Paddle at your own speed, whether you're chasing the dawn, having a lunchtime adventure, or relaxing at dusk.

Top Spots: Visit *Peschiera del Garda* or *Riva del Garda*, where the waters are particularly tranquil and great for novices. If you're more experienced, explore the slightly choppier northern areas of the lake for a more difficult task.

Family-Friendly Fun: Kayaking and paddleboarding are fantastic activities for couples, families, and lone explorers. Rent a two-person kayak for a group adventure, or race your buddies to the next cove.

Pro Tip: Wear quick-drying clothing and pack a waterproof pouch to protect your phone and valuables.

Adventure Awaits at Lake Garda

Lake Garda is more than simply a lovely location; it's an experience waiting to happen. Whether you're diving into canyons, flying above the lake, hiking through beautiful woods, or paddling across placid waterways, this location encourages you to appreciate the great outdoors in all its splendour.

Lake Garda has an adventure for everyone, regardless of skill level or amount of risk-taking. So, lace up your boots, gather your supplies, and let the lake's beauty drive your enthusiasm. With each climb, glide, or paddle, you'll make memories that will keep you going long after your adventure is over.

Day Trips From Lake Garda

While Lake Garda's appeal is unquestionable, its position gives it an ideal starting point for seeing some of northern Italy's most compelling places. From charming cities to high mountains, every day excursion provides a new adventure that is only a short distance away. Whether you're drawn to Verona's romantic alleyways, Venice's dreamy canals, the Dolomites' craggy peaks, or Brescia's cultural riches, these excursions will enhance your Lake Garda experience.

Let's dig into the highlights of four memorable day excursions!

Verona: The City of Romeo and Juliet

Step into a place where history and romance merge harmoniously. Verona, located just an hour from Lake Garda, welcomes you to explore its cobblestone streets and immerse yourself in its timeless beauty. The highlights include

- **Juliet's Balcony:** Experience the wonder of Shakespeare's Romeo and Juliet in the renowned Casa di Giulietta. Take a selfie below the balcony or leave a love note in the courtyard.

- **Piazza delle Erbe:** Originally a Roman forum, this vibrant plaza is today home to cafés, market booths, and Renaissance buildings.
- **Arena di Verona:** This historic amphitheatre, erected in the first century AD, is being used today. If your visit coincides with an opera performance, grasp the opportunity to see the show.

What makes Verona unique? Its combination of Roman remains, mediaeval walls, and dynamic modern activity produces an atmosphere reminiscent of a romantic movie scenario.

Travel Tips: Verona is easily reached by train or vehicle. Allow a whole day to see its ancient monuments and have a leisurely lunch at a trattoria in Piazza Bra.

Venice: A Day by the Canals

A trip to Lake Garda isn't complete without seeing Venice, the "Floating City." Just under two hours away, Venice is a marvel of art, architecture, and waterways waiting to be discovered. Below are the the Must-sees:

- **St. Mark's Square & Basilica:** Start your journey at Venice's renowned centre. Admire the basilica's exquisite mosaics and have a coffee at one of the square's ancient cafés.
- **Rialto Bridge:** This gorgeous architectural treasure provides spectacular views of the Grand Canal and is flanked by businesses offering everything from jewellery to local specialities.
- **Gondola Ride:** Travel around Venice's small canals aboard a gondola. It's a bit of a splurge, but the serene view of the city is amazing.

Why Venice? The city's ethereal beauty and rich history make it one of the world's most popular attractions. Even a day spent traversing its maze of streets seems like entering a live picture.

Travel Tip: To maximise your time in Venice, take an early train from Lake Garda. Wear comfortable shoes; strolling is the greatest way to find secret corners and calm squares.

Dolomite Mountains Excursion

For nature lovers, a day excursion to the Dolomites is essential. This UNESCO World Heritage Site, located just a few hours from Lake Garda, has magnificent peaks, tranquil valleys, and limitless options for adventure. Top experiences includes:

- **Lake Carezza:** Known as the "Rainbow Lake," its vibrant colours mirror the surrounding trees and mountains. It's an easy stop on the road to the Dolomites.
- **Tre Cime di Lavaredo:** This famous trio of peaks is a hiker's heaven. Whether you're prepared for a strenuous walk or a peaceful stroll, the vistas will leave you awestruck.
- **Alpine Villages:** Charming villages such as Cortina d'Ampezzo provide cosy cafés, local crafts, and stunning alpine vistas.

What makes the Dolomites special? The combination of towering limestone cliffs, lush meadows, and charming towns creates a surreal atmosphere.

Travel Tips: Start early to make the most of your time in the mountains. Pack clothing since the weather may change fast, and bring a camera to record the breathtaking view.

Brescia: Rich History and Culture

Brescia, sometimes overshadowed by its more flashy neighbours, is a hidden gem rich in history, art, and culture. It's only an hour away from Lake Garda, making it an ideal destination for a more relaxed but still rewarding day excursion. The following are ley attractions:

- **Santa Giulia Museum:** Housed in a former monastery, this museum contains a wealth of Roman artefacts, mediaeval murals, and Renaissance artwork.
- **Brescia Castle:** Perched on a hill above the city, this well-preserved fortress provides breathtaking vistas and unique displays.
- **Piazza della Loggia:** This Renaissance plaza is the centre of Brescia's old town, flanked with fine buildings and buzzing with local activity.

Why Visit Brescia? The city is a unique combination of historic and contemporary, with a less touristic atmosphere that allows you to enjoy true Italian culture.

Travel Tips: Brescia is well-connected by train and has a more calm pace than larger cities. Enjoy a leisurely meal with local specialities like casoncelli (stuffed pasta) and spiedo Bresciano (meat skewers).

Making the Most of Your Day Trips

Plan ahead: Look up train timetables, opening hours, and must-see sites for your location. Booking tickets in advance might save you time and money.

Pack Smart: Bring necessities such as a reusable water bottle, comfortable shoes, and a lightweight jacket. A compact rucksack is perfect for transporting your essentials while leaving your hands free.

Allow for Spontaneity: While having a plan is important, give yourself time to explore and discover hidden gems—these moments are typically the highlights of your vacation.

Return to Lake Garda in Style: After a day of exploring, unwind with a lakeside aperitivo while recounting your experiences.

Whether you're retracing the paths of star-crossed lovers in Verona, floating through Venice's canals, admiring the raw grandeur of the Dolomites, or discovering Brescia's cultural resources, these day trips enrich your Lake Garda experience. Each place has its own distinct allure, ensuring that your experience is as different as it is memorable.

Seasonal Events & Festivals

Lake Garda is more than simply a beautiful destination for its scenery and activities; it is also a thriving cultural hub with a calendar packed with seasonal events and festivals. Regardless of when you arrive, the lake's cities and villages are alive with celebrations of nature, music, food, and community. From the earliest flowers of spring to the festive glow of winter, Lake Garda provides a unique opportunity to immerse yourself in its traditions and spirit.

Mark your calendars—these events will make your Lake Garda vacation even more memorable.

Spring Flower Festivals

As winter melts and spring arrives, Lake Garda changes into a kaleidoscope of colours. The region's gardens and streets come alive, celebrating the season with floral festivals that highlight the area's natural splendour.

Festa della Primavera (Spring Festival): Held in places like Bardolino and Desenzano, this event celebrates spring with open arms. Expect flower markets, art shows, and live music in scenic locations.

Giardini di Arco (Arco Gardens): Arco, a lovely village on the northern shore, holds a flower and garden festival that attracts both visitors and horticulturists. The festival focuses on rare plant species, creative landscaping, and gardening courses.

Parco Sigurtà Tulip Festival: Located just a short drive from Lake Garda, Parco Sigurtà has one of Europe's biggest tulip displays. Explore its perfectly groomed gardens and marvel at the millions of blooming blooms.

Why Visit in Spring? The air is fresh, the lake's landscape is at its peak, and the people are less. Furthermore, floral festivals give an excellent opportunity to enjoy the outdoors and reconnect with the region's natural beauty.

Summer Music and Opera Events

Summer in Lake Garda is linked with music, ranging from tiny lakeside concerts to big operatic performances in ancient locations. Warm evenings and starlit sky create the ideal setting for outstanding cultural events.

Arena di Verona Opera Festival: Although officially located in Verona, this world-renowned event is a must-see for Lake Garda tourists during the summer. Imagine sitting under the stars in a 2,000-year-old Roman amphitheatre, surrounded by tremendous opera singers' voices.

Riva del Garda Music Festival: This northern town showcases a diverse range of classical, jazz, and contemporary musical acts. Set against the stunning background of the lake and mountains, it's a visual and auditory delight.

Lakeside Concerts: Throughout the summer, many villages on Lake Garda, notably Sirmione and Lazise, organise free evening performances. These include classical quartets and vibrant folk bands, which are frequently presented on old piazzas or near the river.

Why Visit in Summer? The days are long and bright, ideal for exploring the lake during the day and immersing oneself in local culture at night. Summer festivals offer a vibrant, joyous atmosphere that is difficult to resist.

Autumn Food and Wine Festivals

Autumn offers a harvest abundance to Lake Garda, making it the best season for food and wine enthusiasts to come. As the leaves change gold, the area gets together to honour its culinary legacy.

Bardolino Wine Festival: This yearly event, held in October, is a wine lover's dream. Stroll down Bardolino's lakefront promenade, savouring the town's trademark red wine and local delights such as risotto, cheese, and olive oil.

Festa del Tartufo (Truffle Festival): Lake Garda's closeness to truffle-rich regions makes it an ideal location for this autumnal delicacy. Desenzano, for example, hosts events where you may sample meals made with fresh truffles and local wines.

Chestnut and Olive Oil Festivals: Small communities like Garda and Torri del Benaco have festivals to celebrate the flavours of the season. Roasted chestnuts, fresh olive oil, and delicious autumn delicacies are the highlights of these cosy gatherings.

Pumpkin Celebrations in Valeggio sul Mincio: Valeggio, located just south of the lake, offers a wonderful pumpkin festival including substantial soups, ravioli, and other seasonal foods.

Why Visit in Autumn? The crowds have thinned, the weather is lovely, and the festivities revolve around enjoying the region's excellent cuisine and wine. Combine this with the golden hues of the countryside, and you get a truly stunning season.

Winter Christmas Markets

When winter arrives, Lake Garda takes on a festive light. Its cities are adorned with lights, and Christmas markets add warmth and brightness to the cold days.

Lazise Christmas Market: The mediaeval alleyways of Lazise are transformed into a winter paradise, replete with wooden kiosks offering handmade gifts, mulled wine, and holiday sweets such as panettone.

Malcesine Magic: Known for its beautiful splendour, Malcesine is even more charming during the Christmas season. The Christmas market is located against the background of Scaliger Castle, giving a fairytale feel.

Arco Christmas Market: Located on the northern coast, Arco's market is known for its cosy alpine atmosphere. Browse the stalls selling local goods, listen to live music, and drink hot chocolate or spiced cider.

Riva del Garda's Santa Claus Village: This event is ideal for families, with a Santa's grotto, ice skating rink, and holiday shows. Children will enjoy the vibrant décor and activities planned specifically for them.

Why Visit in Winter? The crisp air, festive attitude, and cosy environment make winter in Lake Garda a unique experience. Christmas markets provide a unique opportunity to purchase gifts while also enjoying the region's seasonal flavours.

Tips for Enjoying Seasonal Events

- **Plan Ahead:** Many festivals and events are popular, so book tickets or lodgings in advance, especially during the summer and around Christmas.
- **Dress for the Weather:** Dress accordingly for the weather, whether it's spring showers or winter cold, so you can completely enjoy the festivities without feeling uncomfortable.
- **Engage with Locals:** Seasonal events provide an excellent opportunity to meet

locals and learn about Lake Garda's customs and history.
- **Sample the Flavours:** Each season provides its own gastronomic specialities; don't pass up the opportunity to try something new!

Regardless of when you visit Lake Garda, the region's seasonal festivities offer a lively element of excitement to your experience. From the vibrant energy of spring to the cosy light of winter, these festivals are as much about community and tradition as they are about fun and revelry.

So, which season appeals to your soul? Whether you're drawn to the floral displays of spring, the melodies of summer, the flavours of autumn, or the sparkle of winter, Lake Garda's festivals will leave you with treasured memories and a greater appreciation for this fascinating region.

Sustainable Travel Tips for Lake Garda

Travelling sustainably is more than a fad; it's a thoughtful approach to discover the globe while conserving its beauty for future generations. Lake Garda, with its crystal-clear waters, breathtaking scenery, and lovely cities, is a great location for responsible tourism. During your vacation, you may lessen your environmental effect while also benefiting the local community.

Here's how you may travel responsibly while enjoying your vacation in Lake Garda.

Eco-Friendly Transportation Options

Using greener modes of transportation is one of the simplest ways to reduce your environmental impact. Fortunately, Lake Garda has various alternatives that allow you to explore while remaining environmentally mindful.

Trains & Buses: Arriving at Lake Garda by rail is not only environmentally responsible, but also a beautiful experience. Italy's efficient rail network connects large cities such as Milan, Venice, and Verona with neighbouring communities such as Desenzano del Garda and Peschiera del Garda.

Once there, local buses provided by firms such as ATV or Arriva may transport you to villages surrounding the lake. When feasible, take public transportation—it's an excellent method to decrease emissions while still enjoying the experience.

Cycling Adventures: Lake Garda is a cyclist's paradise, with a vast network of bike roads and trails. Rent a bicycle and ride along the lake's side, soaking in the gorgeous scenery and lessening your dependency on motorised transportation. The recently completed Garda by Bike track is especially spectacular, providing a safe and picturesque route suitable for all ability levels.

Electric Boats: Consider hiring an electric or hybrid boat rather than a standard motorboat to explore the lake from the water. These boats are quieter, produce less pollution, and allow you to explore without disrupting the lake's fragile environment. Many marinas surrounding Lake Garda now provide eco-friendly boat rentals.

Carpooling & Electric Cars: If you must drive, choose a hybrid or electric car. Several automobile rental firms in the region provide environmentally friendly solutions. Additionally, carpooling with other travellers helps minimise the number of automobiles on the road. Look for carpooling options on apps or in local forums.

Supporting Local Businesses

Sustainable travel is about more than simply conserving the environment; it also benefits the local economy and culture. Lake Garda's villages are rich in history, craftsmanship, and culinary traditions, making it simple to buy, dine, and stay nearby.

Shop Locally: Instead of purchasing mass-produced souvenirs, opt for handcrafted items created by local craftsmen. Whether it's olive oil, wine, pottery, or jewellery, buying directly from local producers supports their lives while providing you with a unique souvenir. Markets in communities like Desenzano and Lazise are excellent places to buy genuine, locally created goods.

Eat Locally: Dining at family-run restaurants and agriturismos (farm stays) is a delightful way to help your local community. These restaurants frequently acquire their supplies from surrounding farms, resulting in fresh, seasonal, and sustainable meals. When feasible, go for dishes that feature local specialities like lake fish, Garda olive oil, and Bardolino wine.

Stay Locally: Choose locally owned and operated motels over giant foreign chains. Many boutique hotels, house & breakfasts, and agriturismos provide a genuine experience while reinvesting profits in the community. Look for accommodations that have eco-certifications or practise sustainable techniques.

Join Local Tours: Schedule excursions and activities conducted by local guides. Not only will you learn more about the region's history and culture, but you will also contribute to the local economy. Whether it's a wine tour or a guided walk, locally managed events typically have a reduced environmental effect.

Reducing Plastic Use around the Lake

Lake Garda's beautiful waters are its most valuable resource, and minimising plastic trash is critical to protecting them. Here's how you can participate:

Carry a Reusable Water Bottle: Italy is well-known for its profusion of public water fountains, which can be seen in many cities surrounding Lake Garda. These fountains offer clean, drinking water, allowing you to refill your bottle rather than purchasing single-use plastic bottles. Look for the phrase acqua potabile to ensure it's safe to drink.

Say No to Plastic Bags: Pack a reusable tote bag for outings to local markets or retailers. It's a simple approach to decrease trash and avoid acquiring extra plastic bags throughout your stay.

Go for Sustainable Dining Practices: When dining out or getting takeout, please refuse plastic cutlery, straws, and packaging wherever feasible. Many businesses around Lake Garda are switching to biodegradable or reusable alternatives, so help by carrying your own travel utensils or asking for eco-friendly solutions.

Participate in Clean-Up Efforts: If you're spending the day at the beach or hiking trails, take a time to pick up any litter you see. Some local organisations even organise clean-up events; attending one is a satisfying way to personally help to the lake's preservation.

Final Tips for Traveling Sustainably

Pack Light: The weight of your luggage determines how much gasoline is necessary to deliver it. Pack only what you need and go for multi-functional apparel to decrease the weight of your pack.

Conserve Energy and Water: Be aware of your electricity and water consumption, whether you're staying in a hotel or a vacation rental. Turn off lights, disconnect gadgets, and take shorter showers to reduce your effect.

Respect Nature: When trekking, stick to defined pathways to prevent upsetting wildlife. If you are boating or swimming, make sure your actions do not impair the lake's habitat.

Spread Awareness: Share your experiences with friends and family, and encourage others to use sustainable methods when travelling. The more people embrace responsible tourism, the more favourable the influence on places like Lake Garda.

By following these suggestions, you may enjoy the beauty of Lake Garda while also helping to protect it for future visitors. Sustainable travel does not mean abandoning fun; it means increasing your experience and leaving the areas you visit in better condition than you found them.

Practical Tips for a Smooth Vacation

Planning a vacation to Lake Garda is a thrilling experience, but having a few practical suggestions at your disposal may make a huge difference. Whether it's learning local traditions, recognising the ideal times to travel, or navigating day-to-day necessities, these tips will help you feel prepared and confident. Let's make your Lake Garda holiday as seamless and pleasurable as possible!

Currency, ATMs and Tip Etiquette

Navigating money concerns in a strange nation can be difficult at times, but with this advice, you'll find it much easier around Lake Garda.

Currency: Italy uses the euro (€). Most stores, restaurants, and attractions take credit cards, but it's always a good idea to bring extra cash for minor purchases, such as gelato or market products.

ATMs: ATMs are readily available throughout Lake Garda's municipalities. Look for machines labelled bancomat and utilise those placed within banks for enhanced protection. Check with your bank regarding foreign withdrawal costs to avoid surprises.

Tipping Etiquette: Tipping in Italy is not as common as in other nations, although it is valued for exceptional service.
- In restaurants, a coperto (cover fee) is frequently included, therefore a 5-10% tip is appropriate.
- Taxis often round up to the closest euro.
- Hotel workers, such as porters and housekeepers, would welcome a €1-2 tip.

Insider Tip: Always check your bill for a service fee (servizio incluso), which implies tipping is not required.

Safety Tips for Tourists

Lake Garda is typically a safe place, but being cautious and prepared is essential for a trouble-free trip.

Protect your Belongings: While violent crime is uncommon, pickpocketing can occur in congested settings, particularly in markets or on public transit. Use a crossbody bag with a tight zipper to keep track of your stuff.

Swimming & Boating Safety: The lake's waters are enticing, but safety always comes first. Swim only in approved places, and if you rent a boat, respect local rules and use a life jacket.

Stay Hydrated: Summers may be hot, particularly during outdoor activities. Carry a reusable water bottle and use public water faucets to remain hydrated.

Emergency Numbers:
- The general emergency number is 112.
- Police: 113.
- Medical assistance: 118.

Keep these numbers on your phone just in case.

Tip: If you're trekking or exploring less-traveled regions, notify someone of your plans and bring a fully charged phone with a local SIM or roaming plan.

Language and Common Phrases

Italian is the official language spoken in Lake Garda, and while many residents who work in tourism understand English, learning a few basic words may improve your experience and demonstrate respect for the local culture.

Basic Italian Phrases for Travellers
Greetings:
- Hello: Ciao (informal), Buongiorno (formal)
- Good evening: Buonasera
- Goodbye: Arrivederci

Polite Expressions:
- Please: Per favore
- Thank you: Grazie
- You're welcome: Prego
- Excuse me / Sorry: Mi scusi / Scusa

Dining and Shopping:
- I'd like...: Vorrei...
- How much does it cost?: Quanto costa?
- The check, please: Il conto, per favore
- Delicious!: Delizioso!

Transportation:
- Where is...?: Dov'è...?
- Train station: Stazione ferroviaria
- Ticket: Biglietto

Helpful Words:
- Yes / No: Sì / No
- Bathroom: Bagno
- Water: Acqua

Locals admire guests who try, even if their Italian isn't flawless. A pleasant smile and a welcoming approach may go a long way towards establishing connections.

Tip: Use translation apps or carry a tiny phrasebook for quick reference. It is particularly useful for menus and signage in small towns.

Final Tips for a Smooth Vacation
- **Pack Smartly:** Many villages feature cobblestone streets, so wear comfortable shoes. Also, carry clothing because the weather might vary during the day, particularly in spring and fall.
- **Book Ahead:** Accommodations and popular attractions tend to fill up quickly, especially during peak seasons. To minimise disappointment, reserve your places early.
- **Be Patient:** Life surrounding Lake Garda takes a more relaxed pace. Embrace the slower pace, enjoy each moment, and don't be afraid to change your plans if necessary.

With these practical recommendations in mind, you'll be well-prepared to enjoy your Lake Garda holiday. Every time spent here, from seeing the towns to immersing yourself in the culture, promises to be unforgettable.

Sample Itineraries

Planning the perfect trip to Lake Garda can feel overwhelming with so much to see and do, but don't worry—this guide has you covered. Whether you're craving relaxation, family fun, or a romantic escape, these curated itineraries will help you make the most of your time while keeping the planning stress-free.

A Relaxing 3-Day Lake Garda Escape

This itinerary is perfect if you're looking to unwind and soak in the natural beauty of Lake Garda without rushing.

Day 1: Sirmione's Serenity
- Morning: Start your day with a leisurely breakfast in Sirmione, a town famous for its historic charm. Visit the iconic Scaliger Castle, then stroll to the nearby Grotte di Catullo, where you'll marvel at ancient Roman ruins.
- Afternoon: Enjoy lunch at a lakefront restaurant, savoring fresh fish dishes. Spend your afternoon at the Terme di Sirmione, a luxurious spa offering thermal baths and wellness treatments.

- Evening: As the sun sets, take a quiet lakeside walk and dine in a cozy trattoria with views of the twinkling lake.

Day 2: Exploring Lazise and Bardolino
- Morning: Head to Lazise for a relaxed morning wandering its medieval streets and enjoying the small local market.
- Afternoon: Make your way to Bardolino, known for its vineyards. Indulge in a wine tasting tour, learning about the region's celebrated wines like Bardolino and Chiaretto rosé.
- Evening: Have dinner at a vineyard restaurant and savor a slow evening under the stars.

Day 3: Riva del Garda's Tranquility
- Morning: Drive or take a ferry to Riva del Garda, a picturesque town on the northern end of the lake. Walk along the waterfront and visit the Torre Apponale for panoramic views.
- Afternoon: Relax on one of the pebbly beaches, enjoying the fresh mountain breeze. Treat yourself to gelato from a local shop before returning.

- Evening: End your trip with a farewell dinner at a refined lakeside restaurant, toasting to your relaxing escape.

A Weeklong Adventure Around the Lake

This itinerary offers a balance of exploration, outdoor activities, and cultural experiences to fully immerse you in the wonders of Lake Garda.

Day 1-2: Southern Charm (Sirmione and Desenzano)
- Visit Scaliger Castle and relax in the thermal baths of Sirmione.
- Explore Desenzano's lively piazza and its Roman Villa archaeological site.

Day 3-4: Western Wonders (Gardone Riviera and Limone sul Garda)
- Tour the fascinating Vittoriale degli Italiani in Gardone Riviera.
- Head to Limone sul Garda to explore its famous lemon groves and walk along the Ciclopista del Garda, a breathtaking cycling and walking path over the lake.

Day 5-6: Northern Adventures (Riva del Garda and Monte Baldo)
- Spend a day hiking or cycling around Riva del Garda and enjoy watersports like windsurfing.
- Take the cable car from Malcesine to Monte Baldo for panoramic views and alpine trails.

Day 7: Eastern Exploration (Lazise, Bardolino, and Garda Town)
- Wrap up your week by exploring Lazise's historic center, enjoying Bardolino's wine culture, and walking the scenic promenade of Garda town.

Family-Focused Itinerary
Keep the kids entertained while creating unforgettable family memories with this fun-packed itinerary.

Day 1: Theme Park Fun in Gardaland
- Spend the entire day at Gardaland, one of Europe's top amusement parks. The variety of rides, shows, and themed areas guarantees smiles for all ages.
- End the day with a family-friendly dinner at a casual pizzeria in nearby Peschiera del Garda.

Day 2: Wildlife and Water Play
- Visit Parco Natura Viva, a wildlife park and safari experience where kids can see lions, giraffes, and other animals up close.
- Cool off in the afternoon at Caneva Aquapark, featuring thrilling slides and relaxing lazy rivers.

Day 3: Boat Trip and Beach Time
- Take a boat trip from Bardolino or Garda Town, giving the family a chance to marvel at the stunning lake views.
- Spend the afternoon on a family-friendly beach, such as Lido di Lazise, where the kids can splash around and build sandcastles.

Day 4: Learning and Exploring
- Explore Malcesine Castle, which features interactive exhibits that kids will enjoy.
- Wrap up the day with a gelato-making class, where everyone can create and taste their own frozen treats.

Romance and Luxury: A Couples' Itinerary

This itinerary is perfect for couples seeking intimacy, relaxation, and unforgettable moments.

Day 1: Luxurious Arrival in Sirmione
- Stay at a boutique hotel or luxury resort with a view of the lake. Begin your day with a spa session at Terme di Sirmione.
- Stroll hand-in-hand through the charming streets of Sirmione before enjoying a romantic dinner overlooking the water.

Day 2: Sunset Cruise and Wine Tasting
- Spend the morning exploring Bardolino's vineyards on a private wine tour.
- In the evening, embark on a sunset cruise on the lake, sipping prosecco as the colors of the sky dance on the water.

Day 3: Hidden Gems and Quiet Moments
- Visit the Sanctuary of Madonna della Corona, a peaceful cliffside retreat ideal for reflection and stunning views.
- Find a secluded picnic spot in Garda Town and enjoy local delicacies while soaking up the serenity.

Day 4: Romantic Villages and Farewell
- Explore the romantic streets of Malcesine or Lazise, taking time to stop at cozy cafés and boutique shops.

- End your trip with a candlelit dinner at a fine dining restaurant, toasting to the unforgettable memories you've created together.

Tailor Your Adventure

These itineraries are just starting points, designed to inspire and guide you. Feel free to mix and match activities based on your preferences and travel pace. With so many treasures to discover around Lake Garda, every itinerary is sure to lead to an extraordinary experience.

Conclusion

As you finish this book, imagine yourself standing on the shore of Lake Garda, staring at the sparkling waters that reach to the horizon. This is more than simply a location; it's a mood, a fusion of history, environment, and culture that lingers long after you leave.

Lake Garda is a place that has something for everyone. Whether you've roamed through mediaeval castles in Sirmione, felt the thrill of adventure while paragliding over Monte Baldo, or savoured the velvety richness of a Bardolino wine, every moment here is a story worth telling.

This book aims to demonstrate that Lake Garda is more than simply a collection of charming cities and stunning landscapes; it is an experience of contrasts. The exhilaration of crowded marketplaces contrasts with the tranquility of a sunset sail. It's the joy of kids in Gardaland and the beautiful serenity of a secret picnic location for two. It's the exuberant clink of drinks in a vineyard and the quiet awe of old ruins.

The essential beauty of Lake Garda is that it allows you to create your own trip. For families, it's a playground where both children and adults may enjoy exploration. Couples will find a canvas painted with romance, from spa getaways to cosy stroll through lovely villages. For adrenaline seekers, it's a doorway to outdoor excursions that will get your heart racing and your emotions flying.

Lake Garda welcomes all types of travellers to calm down and completely immerse themselves in its scenery and culture. You'll discover that it's more than simply seeing; it's about feeling. The smooth lapping of waves against the coast, the earthy perfume of olive trees, the ring of a church bell in a peaceful village—all of these nuances combine to create a symphony that is entirely your own.

Even when you pack your luggage to go, the aura of Lake Garda lingers. It's in the flavours you tried, the laughs you had, and the peaceful moments you discovered. You'll keep its warmth in your heart as a remembrance of a place where time pauses, beauty blooms, and memories are created.

So, whether you're planning a return or reflecting on your time there, Lake Garda will always be waiting—ready to welcome you back with open arms and limitless possibilities. After all, the enchantment of Lake Garda transcends time; it is timeless.

Printed in Great Britain
by Amazon